On Foot in Sonoma

Twelve Walks in the Valley of the Moon

Arthur Dawson
and
Rebecca Lawton

Kulupi Press
Glen Ellen, California

For Jill, who shares my journey, and whose love and companionship have shown me many wonderful and unexpected paths.

—AWD

For my father, whose diligent work helps preserve the natural and historical Sonoma and whose intrepid outings inspired my own.

—RCL

Maps and trail mapping by Ryno Mapping,
www.rynomapping.com
Cover design by Lisa Fortino
Photography by Arthur Dawson, Rebecca Lawton,
and Grace Svitek
Technical, electronic, and moral support
by the Sonoma Ecology Center
Special thanks to Sonoma County GIS and the Sonoma
Ecology Center GIS/GPS Project for map data

Front cover: Sonoma Valley Regional Park (Walk # 5)
Back cover: Bigleaf maple, *Acer macrophyllum*. Sonoma Valley

Orders and correspondence should be addressed to:

Kulupi Press
5026 Warm Springs Road
Glen Ellen, CA 95442
www.kulupi.com

ISBN: 0-9661867-1-0

First printing, March 2004
Printed on recycled paper

10 9 8 7 6 5 4 3 2 1

Contents

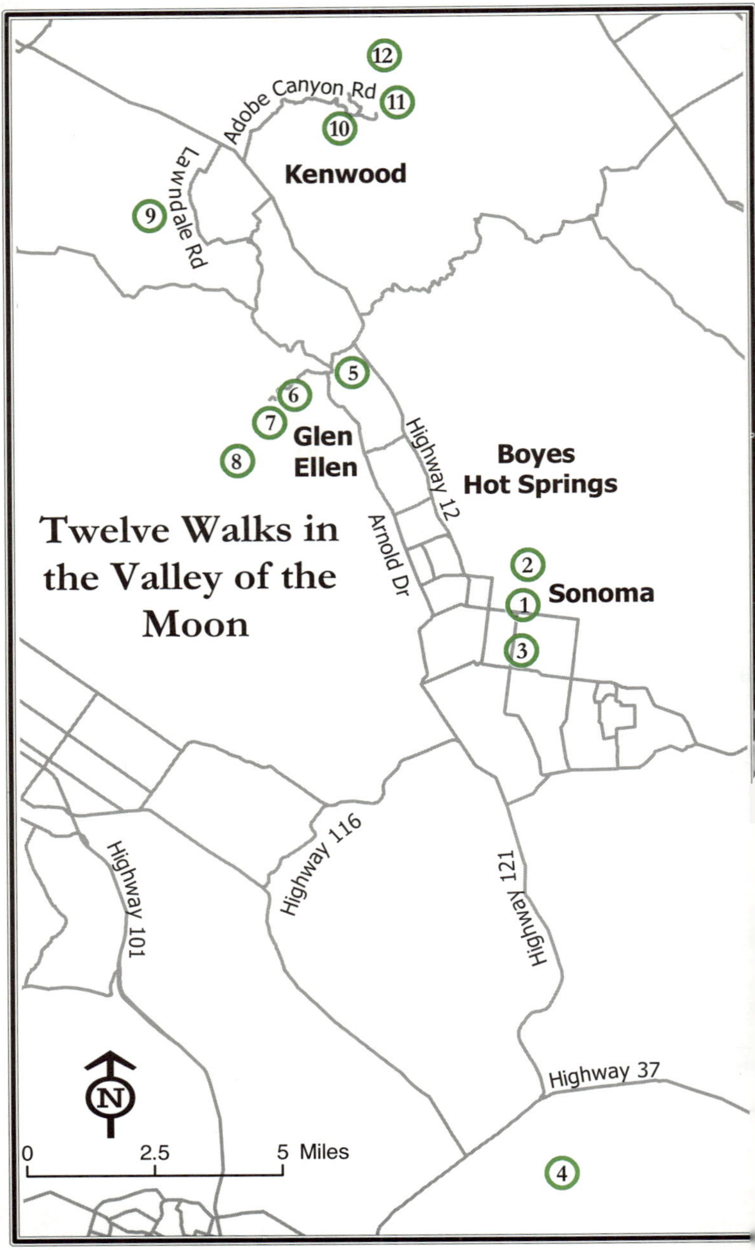

Twelve Walks in the Valley of the Moon
Kenwood
Adobe Canyon Rd
Lawndale Rd
Glen Ellen
Boyes Hot Springs
Sonoma
Highway 12
Arnold Dr
Highway 116
Highway 121
Highway 101
Highway 37
N
0
2.5
5 Miles
1
2
3
4
5
6
7
8
9
10
11
12

About this Book

Sonoma Valley is well known as a fabulous place to visit, with its historic downtown, rural setting, and world-class wineries. Yet those of us lucky enough to live here know these features are only part of the valley's allure. With four state parks, several county parks, city-owned trails, and a national wildlife refuge, Sonoma offers outstanding opportunities to enjoy the great outdoors. Whether it's the song of a hidden waterfall, a hundred-mile view to the snowcapped Sierras, the massive presence of an old-growth redwood, or the flight of an osprey over a tidal marsh, Sonoma abounds with natural treasures just waiting to be discovered.

On Foot in Sonoma is designed to introduce both visitors and locals to Sonoma's richest outdoor experiences, places that offer beauty, solace, awe, and inspiration. The walks in this book range from hour-long strolls to half-day hikes and can easily be combined with visits to other Sonoma attractions. Take your pick from the easy, moderate, and challenging walking options available. At the end of each chapter is a map showing the route and numbered features mentioned in the text. Many chapters have options to shorten or lengthen the walk if desired.

Go at your own pace, go alone or with a friend, but definitely go—and, with this book as your guide, may you find the going rewarding and fun!

Before You Go

Venturing into the outdoors has inherent dangers—sunburn, poison oak, and deer ticks being among the most common nuisances in Sonoma Valley. Long sleeves and pants are good protection against these hazards, and wearing a hat and sunscreen is also advised. Carry drinking water and wear sturdy shoes and comfortable clothes when you embark on a day's journey. Layers of clothing are preferable—they allow changes in response to varying weather conditions. After your walk, check yourself for ticks.

Within the last few years, mountain lions, black bears, rattlesnakes, Chinook salmon, coyote, bobcat, fox, beaver, and mink have all been seen in Sonoma Valley. If you're lucky enough to see wild animals, please observe them quietly and unobtrusively—remember you're a guest in their home. If you come across a rattlesnake, stop immediately and then slowly back away. Trail signboards also have recommendations about how to behave when meeting our wild residents. Be smart!

Please note that dogs are not allowed on state park trails, in the San Pablo Bay National Wildlife Refuge, or on the Sonoma Overlook Trail, for the very good reason that domestic animals are not compatible with wild ones. Enjoy taking your pets on leash where they are allowed—on the walks in town and on regional park trails. The Sonoma Valley Regional Park also has a fenced dog park where your pet can run free.

More Information

A stop at the Visitor's Bureau at 453 First Street East on the historic Sonoma Plaza is helpful, especially if you're making your first trip to the valley. The bureau can give current answers about meals and lodging, visitor attractions, and upcoming events. Call (707) 996-1090.

For anyone choosing a walk in Sonoma Valley's state parks, more information can be found at www.parks.sonoma.net, or by calling California State Parks in Sacramento at (800) 777-0369. Each park also has a visitors' center that is well worth a visit. Hours of the centers can vary greatly—check ahead by calling the California State Parks number.

Further information about the San Pablo Bay National Wildlife Refuge is available at www.fws.gov or at (800) 344-WILD. Learn more about the Sonoma Valley Regional Park at www.sonoma-county.org/parks/pksonoma.htm or by calling Operations at (707) 565-2041.

Safety Note

Kulupi Press does not guarantee the safety of any individual or group visiting or walking in Sonoma Valley or elsewhere. Remember that, as in life in general, you go at your own risk. We have described and mapped the areas and trails shown in this book to the best of our abilities, but changing conditions will warrant modification of instructions and depictions in future versions of *On Foot in Sonoma.* If you have suggestions for a second edition of this book, please write the authors c/o Kulupi Press, 5026 Warm Springs Road, Glen Ellen, California 95442.

Individual trail maps are at the end of each chapter.

1

A Walk on the Town

Sonoma Plaza to Lachryma Montis

2 ½ miles/Moderate/1 hour to half day

This gentle 3-mile stroll is a charming way to experience downtown Sonoma. The walk offers a little of everything—wine tasting, fresh air, flower gardens, and history—all within the city's intimate weave of urban and rural landscapes. Although you could knock this walk off in an hour, we recommend an open-ended schedule that allows plenty of time to sample the many pleasures you'll encounter and the opportunity for a little serendipity along the way. Many of the little courtyards off Sonoma's plaza warrant exploring, as do the surprising number of historic buildings and museums in this unexpectedly rich walking exploration.

Getting There: We recommend parking in the lot behind the Sonoma Barracks. The entrance to the barracks parking is on First Street East, just north of the Sonoma Plaza. Or park at the plaza but be aware of posted time limits.

1 Begin at the **mission bell** opposite the northeast corner of the plaza. Behind the bell is Mission San Francisco Solano de Sonoma, founded in 1823 by Padre José Altimira. The small museum inside deserves a visit. The museum and mission are part of a State Historic Park that includes the Sonoma Barracks and General Mariano G. Vallejo's home, all open to the public from 10 a.m. to 5 p.m. for the cost of a single admission. Just up First Street East, along the sidewalk beside the chapel, is a memorial to the hundreds of native people who died and are buried here.

2 Cross First Street East and you'll find yourself in front of the **Sonoma Barracks**, constructed by General Vallejo in 1836. Next to the barracks is the Toscano Hotel, built by German immigrant Martin Nathanson in the 1850s. Tours of the historic hotel are led Saturday, Sunday, and Monday from 1 p.m. to 4 p.m. Across the street in the plaza itself is a monument to the Bear Flag revolt in 1846.

Continue west on Spain Street. On this block you'll have the chance to visit the Sonoma Cheese Factory, Swiss Hotel, and many small shops. Cross First Street West, turn left, and cross Spain Street. Soon you'll come to

3 the **Salvador Vallejo adobe**, also built during the 1830s.

Salvador was Mariano's younger brother and right-hand man and is said to have been a rough character.

At the end of the block, turn left and cross First Street West.
4 Sonoma's **city hall** is halfway down the street, nestled in the center of the plaza. Here the plaza adjoins Broadway, laid out by General Vallejo when he surveyed Sonoma in 1835.

At the next corner, cross First Street East. Turn left, passing the reconstructed brick building that once housed Pinelli Hardware. A few more steps bring you to the historic **Sebastiani**
5 **Theatre**, which continues to show movies and host live performances.

Coming to the corner of First Street East and Spain Street, you'll find yourself across the
(1) street from the **mission bell** where you began.

Turn right on East Spain Street, soon passing
6 the two-story **Blue Wing adobe**, perhaps California's first hotel north of the bay. On your left you'll see an open pasture and may spot a horse or two.

Cross Second Street East and continue along East Spain. After passing a few houses, you'll see a ring of redwood trees enclosing **Trinity**
7 **Episcopal Church's labyrinth**. It's open to the public and free of charge. To walk the labyrinth, continue down the sidewalk to a paved path veering right and leading toward the church buildings. Follow the path back toward the labyrinth and its redwood grove.

When East Spain Street dead ends at Fourth Street East, turn left. Across the street is the Sebastiani tasting room, open from 10 a.m. to 5 p.m. daily. Continue up Fourth Street East until you see the beginning of **Sonoma's bike**
8 **path** on the left. (Picnic tables are available to the right, down Lovall Valley Road.) Take a left onto the bike path. If you're lucky enough to be here in mid to late summer, you can pick ripe blackberries at many spots along this popular path.

Soon you'll reach a large garden area
9 called **The Patch**. Produce from The Patch is sold at a stand just up the next cross street, Second Street East. Vella Cheese Factory is a few steps in the other direction (to the left).

10 After the bike path crosses First Street East, it enters **Depot Park** (public restroom on the right). The Depot Museum, housed in the rebuilt Sonoma train station, has excellent exhibits on local history (open Wednesday through Sunday, 1 p.m. to 4:30 p.m.).

(1) **Easy Option:** From Depot Park, turn left on First Street East and return to the **mission bell**. Round-trip 1 7/8 miles.

11 Continue along the path, crossing First Street West. Soon you'll find yourself in the wide-open spaces of General Vallejo's former estate. Where the bike path crosses the General's tree-lined driveway, turn right to his Victorian home. Vallejo named his property **Lachryma Montis**, Latin for "Mountain Tear," after a large spring that once supplied water both to his estate and the town of Sonoma. You'll find the grounds pleasant and quiet, with picnic tables, tranquil gardens, and turtles basking in the General's pond.

(10) When you're ready to leave this idyllic place, retrace your steps to **Depot Park**. Turn right just before the Depot Museum onto a paved path that passes the city's popular pétanque court. The barracks parking lot is visible directly ahead.

Extended Option: Add the Sonoma Overlook Trail (page 17) by turning right on First Street West (just west of the Depot Museum) and walking about ¼ mile to the Mountain Cemetery entrance. This extension makes a wonderful outing of about 6 ½ miles.

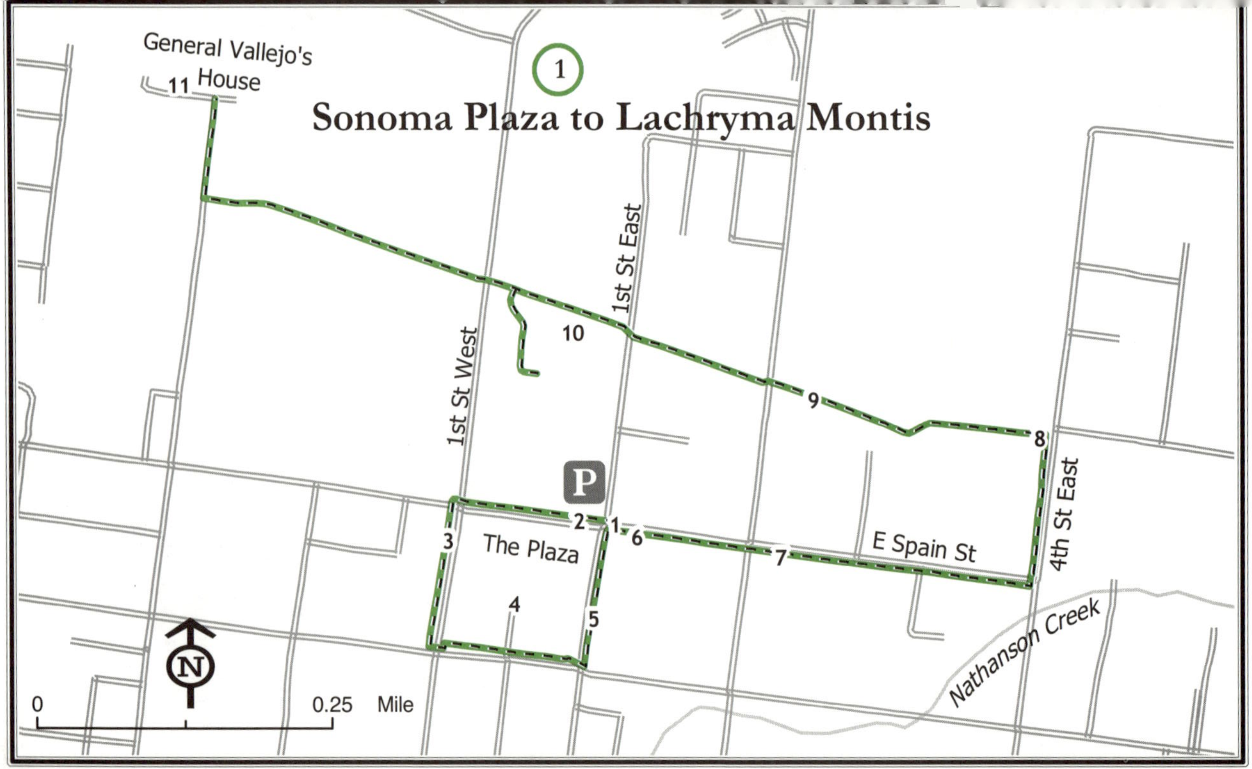

1
Sonoma Plaza to Lachryma Montis
General Vallejo's House
11
10
9
8
1st St West
1st St East
4th St East
E Spain St
The Plaza
P
2
1
6
7
3
4
5
Nathanson Creek
N
0
0.25 Mile

2

The Citizens' Open Space

Sonoma Overlook Trail

2 7/8 miles/Moderate/1 hour

Stunning views of the valley and a gentle climb through open space near the heart of downtown are the rewards of this hike. The Sonoma Overlook Trail traverses a hillside that is under the stewardship of the City of Sonoma, whose citizens voted overwhelmingly in the 1990s to keep the property undeveloped. Community support for hiker-only access led to the creation of the Overlook Trail. The nearly 3-mile loop up the hillside and down through Mountain Cemetery has it all—views, historic interest, community pride, and the solace of oak woodland.

For walkers only; closed to pets, horses, and bicycles.

Getting There: Starting from the Sonoma Plaza (walkers starting at the plaza will add a mile to the hike), go north on First Street West, which runs along the plaza's west side (don't confuse it with First Street East). Pass Spain Street and Depot Park on the right. About 0.5 mile from the plaza, just before the road starts climbing into the hills, turn right and park just outside the gates of the Mountain Cemetery. You'll see a trail sign at the edge of the parking area with a map and information about the trail and its flora and fauna.

The trail begins near the parking lot signboard,
climbs a grassy slope, and enters the woods.
The cemetery and war memorial are on your
right as the trail stays close to the bottom of a
little canyon. Soon the trail turns right, crosses
1 the **canyon bottom**, and begins switchbacking
gently up the other side through patches of
shady forest and open hillsides. The view gets
a little wider, stretching toward the southwest,
each time you come to one of these openings.

Many outcroppings of basalt and other volcanic rocks attest to the fiery birth of these hills. Rich volcanic soils are one reason grape vines in Sonoma and Napa Valleys produce such top-quality fruit. In the late 19th and early 20th centuries, this hillside would have rung with the sound of hammers and chisels as stonecutters produced millions of basalt cobblestones used to pave city streets all over northern California.

2 Eventually you come to a **trail junction** with a
sign reading "Upper Meadow Loop/Toyon

Road Trailhead." The trail to the right leads to the upper part of the cemetery.

3 Stay left on the Upper Meadow Trail and climb to another **trail intersection**, the beginning of the Upper Meadow Loop. You can turn right or left to begin a 3/8-mile loop around the meadow. From here, all of lower Sonoma Valley lies at your feet. Lupine, poppies, mule's ears, and other wildflowers are abundant here in the spring, their bright colors set against green hills and dark outcroppings of basalt.

4 Midway through the loop, at its southwest side, you'll find a **stone bench** dedicated to the memory of local son Scott Evans, "who loved to view his world from on high." Look for the hiker's register in a plastic container tied near the bench. The comments and drawings on nature, life, and politics from visitors of all ages are a highlight of this walk. Be sure to add your own voice to the chorus.

Looking to the right from Scott's bench, you can see west across Sonoma Valley to the long, sloping ridge of Sonoma Mountain. To the southwest, you'll see a pass in the mountain's ridge. Sometimes called Tolay Gap, this is where Father Altimira first entered the valley in 1823 on his expedition to found the Sonoma Mission. A little more to the south are the distant skyscrapers of San Francisco and sometimes a view of the fog sitting in the financial district. Directly south is a nearer view down Sonoma's own Broadway and over the town's neighborhoods, churches, playing fields, roadways, and the vineyards beyond.

Continue on the path until it brings you back to the Upper Meadows Loop **trail**
(3) **intersection**. From there retrace your path to
(2) the **trail junction** and Toyon Road Trailhead signpost and turn left.

5 When you reach pavement at **Toyon Road,** turn right and downhill through the cemetery. Turn right on Willow (no sign), then left on Laurel Lane, past General Vallejo's grave. Continue toward the cemetery gate and soon you'll arrive back at the Lower Trailhead parking lot.

2
Sonoma Overlook Trail
Norrbom Rd
3
4
2
1
5
Toyon Rd
Circle Dr
Vallejo's Grave
Laurel
First St West
Sonoma
P
2nd St East
N
0
0.25 Mile

3

The Wild Side of the City

Nathanson Creek Trail

2 ¼ miles/Easy/1 hour

The Nathanson Creek Trail follows a wooded stream alive with wildlife and birdsong, as well as quiet back streets lined with historic homes. In an impressive effort led by environmentalist Christy Vreeland, the trail was built in a multiyear project of the Sonoma Ecology Center. Christy's vision and hard work paid huge rewards: the trail provides rare access to a surprisingly wild tributary of Sonoma Creek within city limits. Mountain lions are occasionally sighted on Nathanson. The creek is also the valley's most popular salmon-viewing spot: after a many-year hiatus, Chinook salmon spawned in this stream in 2000, just a block from the Sonoma Plaza. A heartening sight, they reared successfully and have been seen several times since, usually in mid or late December.

Getting There: From the Sonoma Plaza, go south on Broadway just over a mile, past Sonoma Valley High and Adele Harrison Middle Schools, to the light at Napa Road. Turn left on Napa Road. Go 0.3 mile, turn left onto Larkin Street, then left again on Dewell Drive. Follow Dewell to Nathanson Creek Park on the left. Park on the street, observing the "No Parking" signs in the cul-de-sac at Dewell and Fine.

The paved trail, marked "Bike Path," begins to the right of the Nathanson Creek Park sign and playground. Willow, black walnut, and ash trees grow along the creek in this area, creating a relatively lush riparian zone. As you walk, you'll also see California buckeyes and hear birdsong mixed with the sounds of city traffic.
1 Soon the trail emerges into a **large, open field** with a wide view toward the Mayacamas Mountains. In the spring you may see expanses of lupine and California poppies blooming here.

After five or so minutes of walking, you'll pass
2 a **bridge** on the left. Continue straight (neither crossing the bridge nor taking the paved path to the right), past a drinking
3 fountain and basketball court. Pass a **second bridge** on the left.

Continue through a gap in the chain-link fence,
4 pass a **third bridge**, and reach MacArthur Street. Cross MacArthur and turn left. Immediately cross Nathanson Creek on a
5 bridge and turn right on **Austin Avenue**. Nathanson Creek now stays out of sight as you walk the length of Austin. Continue north, past homes with well-tended gardens, crossing Chase and France Streets. Watch for a **large**
6 **oak tree** on the right side of Austin Avenue. This tree has probably been here since well before the founding of the Sonoma Mission in 1823.

Just before Patten Street, you momentarily rejoin Nathanson Creek. Turn right on Patten and left on Second Street East. Pass several large, nineteenth-century mansions and come
7 to an old **stone bridge**. If you come in December, look closely at the pool just down-

stream from the bridge; you may see Chinook salmon spawning here.

Retrace your steps for a 2 ¼-mile roundtrip.

Extended Options: Continue to the
(7) Sonoma Plaza from the **stone bridge** by turning left on East Napa Street. Circle the Plaza, then retrace your steps back to Nathanson Creek Park, for a walk of 3 miles total.

For a 6-mile foot tour of Sonoma, combine this walk with "A Walk on the Town" on page 11. From the **stone**
(7) **bridge** go left on East Napa Street, then right on First Street East to the Sonoma Mission at the northeast corner of the Plaza, where "A Walk on the Town" begins.

3
Nathanson Creek
Trail
E Napa St
Patten St
Nathanson Creek
France St
Austin Ave
2nd St East
Chase St
1st St West
MacArthur St
Broadway
7
6
5
4
3
2
1
P
N
0
0.25
Mile

4

Sonoma's Big Sky Country

Lower Tubbs Island Trail

8 1/8 miles/Moderate/3 hours

Exceptional birdwatching, wide-open vistas across San Pablo Bay to Mount Tamalpais and Mount Diablo, and a restored tidal marsh are the highlights of this level hike. The Lower Tubbs Island Trail is within the San Pablo Bay National Wildlife Refuge, established in 1974 for the protection of endangered species and migratory birds. Refuge land was acquired with the help of The Nature Conservancy in an effort to restore the tidal marshes, which have been reduced to a fraction of their historical size around the bay. Nearby water and an onshore breeze keep temperatures here comfortable even on days that are hot inland. However, the lack of shade on this hike makes preparation for sun exposure essential.

Due to protected wildlife, the refuge is closed to pets and fishing. The refuge trails are ideal for mountain biking if the ground isn't muddy from recent rains.

Getting There: Starting at the Sonoma Plaza, drive south on Broadway (Highway 12) for 3.7 miles. Turn right on Highway 121 (toward San Francisco). Drive 0.7 mile to the four-way stop at the intersection with Highway 116. Turn left and continue 6.5 miles (you're still on Highway 121) to Highway 37. Turn left on 37 toward the City of Vallejo. In about 0.7 mile, just past a large expanse of open water, take the first available right turn, which leads you into the refuge parking lot. There are no facilities at the parking area except a signboard with notices posted about the refuge. The open water nearby is an excellent waterfowl viewing area. You may see many of the refuge's common sea and diving birds—cormorants, western grebes, scaups, and buffleheads—preening and feeding.

From the lot, walk south on the dirt refuge road. Fairly steady hiking on level terrain beside the levees of Tolay Creek will take you past cultivated fields on the left and the marsh with its salt-tolerant pickleweed and cordgrass on the right. After 3/8 mile you
1 reach a **picnic table**.

The refuge road now veers to the southeast. If you hear distant, popping sounds, it's gunfire from a hunting club and nothing to
2 worry about. Soon you'll come to a **junction**

with another dirt road on the left posted with a "No Trespassing" sign. The road turns southwest for about ¾ mile. As the road curves back toward the southeast, you'll pass a
3 **pumping station** covered in sheet metal on the left.

Continue on the trail as it heads southeast for 5/8 of a mile. Pass a dirt road on the left and
4 reach an **information kiosk** and wildlife viewing area. You may see osprey, pelicans, snowy egrets, sanderlings, American egrets, long-billed curlews, and willets. The occasional jackrabbit darts across the road, and there are glimpses of tiny mammals such as the salt marsh harvest mouse.

Easy Option: Retrace your steps from here back to the parking lot, making this a 5½-mile walk.

Turn right at the beginning of the loop. The cultivated fields have faded away and you're surrounded by salt marsh and tidal sloughs.

A half mile of walking brings you near a cluster of **red**
5 **barns**. The trail curves around
6 to the **shore of San Pablo**

Bay and follows it east for a while before turning north.

7 Stay left where a **side road** comes in on the right.

(4) Another 3/8 of a mile brings you back to the **information kiosk**. Retrace your steps from here back to the parking lot for a round-trip walk of 8 1/8 miles.

A Note on the Return Drive: Leaving the refuge, you must turn right on Highway 37. Drive 3 miles (crossing the bridge over Sonoma Creek) and turn left at the sign for Skaggs Island. After making the left on Skaggs Island Road, turn around in the large dirt pullout. From the stop sign at the Skaggs Island Road/Highway 37 intersection, turn right onto Highway 37. Drive 3.8 miles and turn right on Highway 121, which will take you back to Sonoma.

Pickleweed, a common plant in the tidal marshes

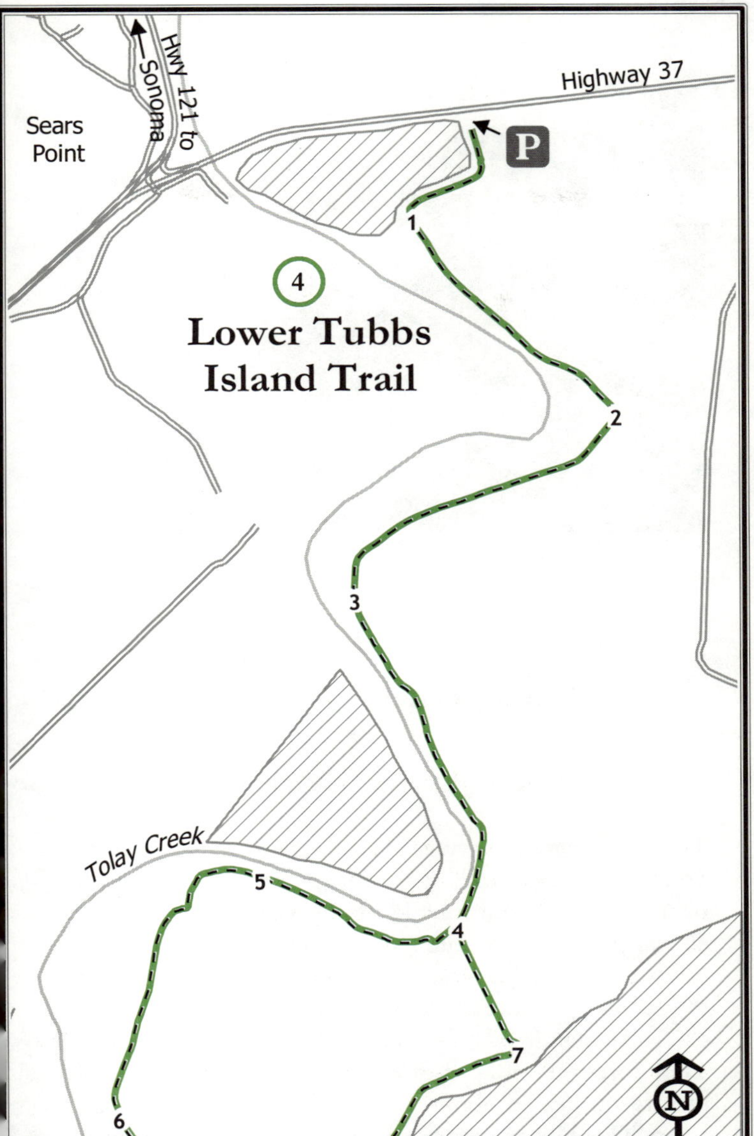

Highway 37
Hwy 121 to Sonoma
Sears Point
P
4
Lower Tubbs Island Trail
1
2
3
4
5
6
7
Tolay Creek
San Pablo Bay
N
0
0.25
0.5
Mile

5

Woodpeckers' Paradise

Sonoma Valley Regional Park Loop

3 miles/Moderate/1 to 2 hours

This hidden gem provides great views from the heart of Sonoma Valley's wildlife corridor. A swath of natural habitat through the middle of the valley, the corridor allows passage of wildlife from Sonoma Mountain on the west to the Mayacamas on the east. In the hills at the center of the corridor, the regional park has extensive stands of blue oak, madrone, and manzanita. The forest is a paradise for woodpeckers on a picturesque ridge above the creekside town of Glen Ellen. This hike covers both easy and rigorous strolling: some paths are paved and mild; others rocky and steep. It's a lovely walk any time of year, but it may be best on a warm spring day in March or April when wildflowers blanket the hillsides.

Getting There: From the Sonoma Plaza, follow Highway 12 north through the Boyes Hot Springs area, passing Verano Avenue, Boyes Boulevard, and Agua Caliente Road. About 1.7 miles beyond Madrone Road, at the top of a rise, is a California Department of Forestry fire station on the left. One tenth of a mile beyond, also on the left, is the entrance to the Sonoma Valley Regional Park. Follow the entrance road a short distance to the parking lot. There's a parking fee. (Annual county park passes are available.)

At the far end of the parking lot is a drinking fountain and restroom. Just beyond is the beginning of a paved trail. Follow this trail for about 200 yards (passing a dirt road heading steeply uphill) to a dirt road marked with a **trail**
1 **sign**. Turn left onto this trail, then stay right at each fork as you curve around to the crest of the ridge.

> **Easy Option:** Stay on the paved trail, following it as far as you wish. Benches and several tables offer many resting and picnic spots along the way. Then retrace your steps to the parking lot for an easy walk of anywhere from ¼ mile to 2 ½ miles.

2 Reaching the **hilltop**, you'll be rewarded with sweeping views up and down Sonoma Valley. Benches on either side of the trail make nice resting spots. To the west stretches the long

ridge of Sonoma Mountain. To the east are the Mayacamas Mountains: much of the area visible from here was swept by huge wildfires in 1923 and 1964. Both fires blackened about 10,000 acres, destroyed homes in Boyes Hot Springs area, and threatened the town of Sonoma. Old-timers say you could read at night in Glen Ellen by the light of the flames.

From the hilltop, follow the trail along the ridge, soon reaching a four-way intersection. Several paths criss-cross here, all following the ridgeline. Keep right. Soon you'll spot a barbed-wire fence above the trail—keep the fence on your left.

3 A few minutes of walking bring you to a **marked trail** heading off to the right. This spot is popular with acorn woodpeckers. Even if you don't see or hear any, the many round holes drilled in dead limbs

and logs attest to their presence. The woodpeckers store acorns in these holes.

The trail has three forks here. Take the middle fork (neither cross the barbed-wire fence to the left nor take the signed trail to the right). Stay on the trail along the north side of the ridge, through a forest of oak, madrone, and manzanita, with occasional views of upper Sonoma Valley and Bennett Mountain.

4 Pass **another trail** taking off to the right. Stay left on the upper trail, making a short, steep ascent, followed by a rocky downhill with views of Sonoma Mountain. At the bottom you enter an open meadow and quickly reach the paved trail again.

5 Turn right on the **paved trail**, which follows the bed of one of the railroads that used to serve Glen Ellen. Depending on the season, you may hear Sonoma Creek gurgling below. Across the creek are some large buildings now known as Jack London Village. General Vallejo built a sawmill there in 1839, on Asbury Creek, to harvest the redwoods and Douglas fir on Sonoma Mountain.

In about a half mile, the paved trail brings you under the deep shade of madrone and bay trees
6 and passes a **dirt trail** on the left. Keep on the paved trail, soon reaching a seasonal streambed. The trail parallels it, heading upstream. In a few
7 minutes you come to a pair of **trail junctions**, with dirt paths taking off to the left and right.

Stay on the paved trail as it winds along the bottom of this little valley, passing benches and a picnic table. Soon the trail emerges into an open grassy area studded with blue oaks, climbs a small rise, and curves to the left, bringing you back to the parking lot.

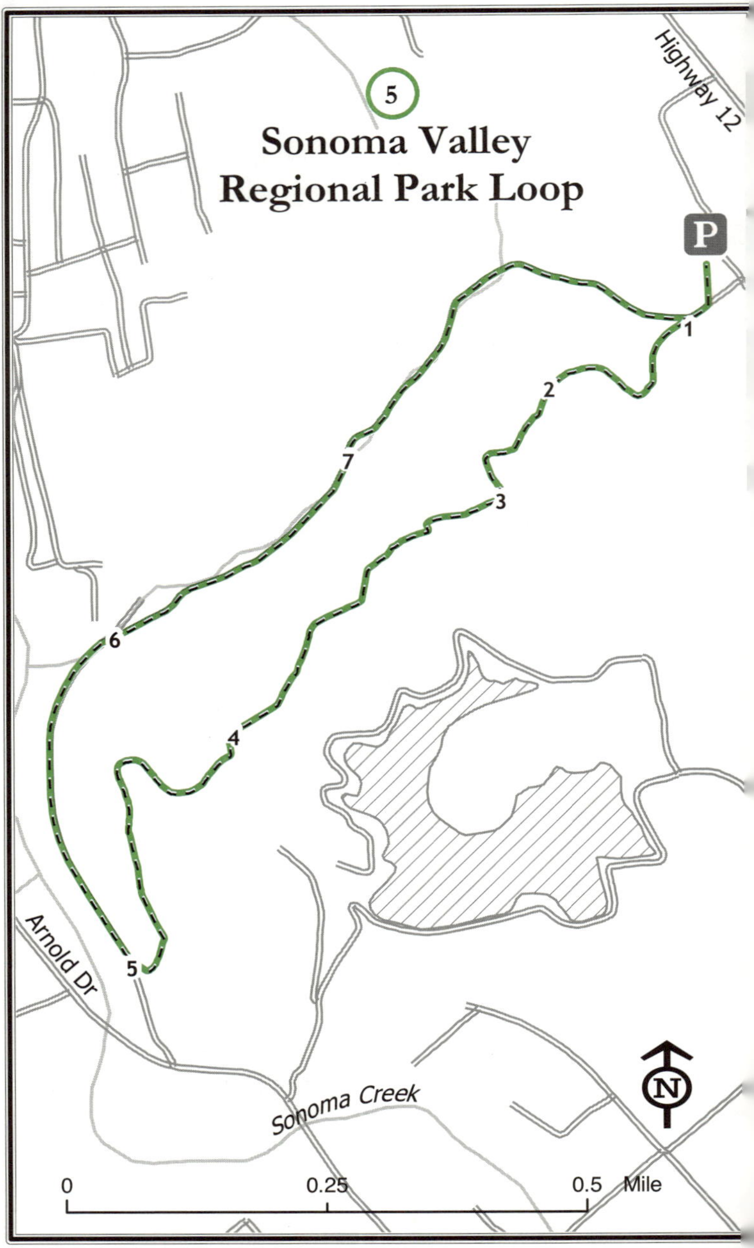
5
Sonoma Valley
Regional Park Loop
Highway 12
P
1
2
3
4
5
6
7
Arnold Dr
Sonoma Creek
N
0
0.25
0.5 Mile

6

A Castle in the Woods

Wolf House Trail

1 3/8 miles/Easy/1 hour

This short hike leads through a mixed forest of oak, madrone, Douglas fir, and redwood to Wolf House, Jack London's dream home. Follow this trail for an excellent introduction to the area's history, streams, and woods. Between international jaunts, London made Glen Ellen his home, and the beautiful state park named for him is a crown jewel of Sonoma Valley.

Getting There: Starting at the Sonoma Plaza, take Highway 12 north through the Boyes Hot Springs area, passing Verano Avenue, Boyes Boulevard, and Agua Caliente Roads. Four and a half miles from the plaza, turn left on Madrone Road. Follow Madrone about 1 mile to its end and turn right on Arnold Drive, following it for 2 miles into Glen Ellen. Turn left on London Ranch Road (just before the main bridge) and follow it 1 ½ miles to Jack London State Park. After paying your entrance fee at the kiosk, immediately turn left into the lower parking lot, where there are restrooms and picnic tables.

From the far end of the parking lot, walk up the paved walkway toward the House of Happy Walls. Don't miss this intriguing collection of memorabilia from London's life housed in the home of his widow and "she-mate," Charmian. Inside are photographs of London at work, books by and about him, and furniture custom built for the never-inhabited Wolf House. On weekends evocative melodies played by professional musicians at London's own piano carry from the open windows of this beautiful stone building.

1 Just below the house you'll see a **trail sign** for London's grave and the Wolf House.

Turn right and begin with an easy downhill stroll through a forest of Douglas fir, toyon, and madrone. In just over ¼ mile, you'll reach a
2 **junction** with the paved Wolf House service road.

Turn left on the service road and follow it as it climbs a gentle hill. At the top of the hill is a
3 **trail junction** where a 150-yard detour to the left will bring you to the knoll containing Jack and Charmian London's graves and those of the pioneer Greenlaw children.

A few minutes' stroll downhill brings you to the forest clearing where the ruins of Jack London's
4 dream home, the **Wolf House**, still stand. Here he planned to finish his days, in a mansion of basalt and redwood above the singing waters of Asbury Creek. London spared no expense in the building, with its double-thick walls, earthquake - proof concrete slab, and outdoor pool. But he never lived here, for it burned just before he was to move in. It was rumored that an arsonist was responsible, but fire specialists who studied the site in 1995 believe that oil-soaked rags left in a corner spontaneously combusted and set Wolf House ablaze.

Today silence settles reverently on London's enduring walls, the beauty of the place transcending the splendor of the building. Light streams through the redwoods; in spring, tall grass and purple vetch line the roads as California buckeyes bloom like glowing candles. Hawks and vultures circle the site, hunting and scavenging. One can understand London's urge to leave the busy streets of Oakland for this writing refuge, where nothing but the sound of the creek breaks the quiet.

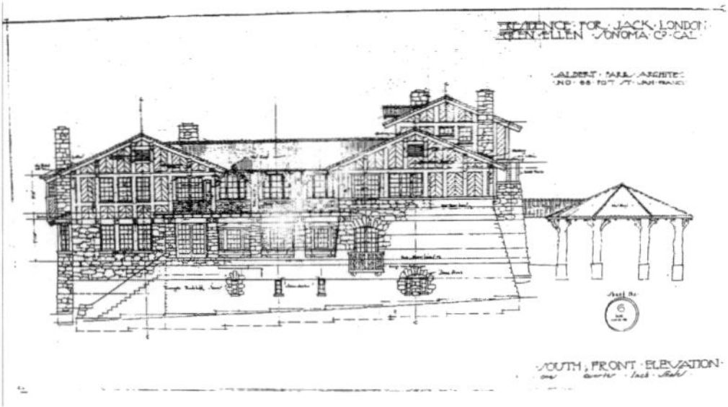

(2) On your return, retrace your steps just over ¼ mile to the **junction** with the path leading to the House of the Happy Walls. Although you can turn right here if you wish, we recommend making a loop by continuing straight on the service road. The distance is the same, and the service road offers a picturesque view of vineyards and Sonoma Mountain that you'll miss if you return on the path.

5 A few minutes' walk brings you back to the **parking lot.**

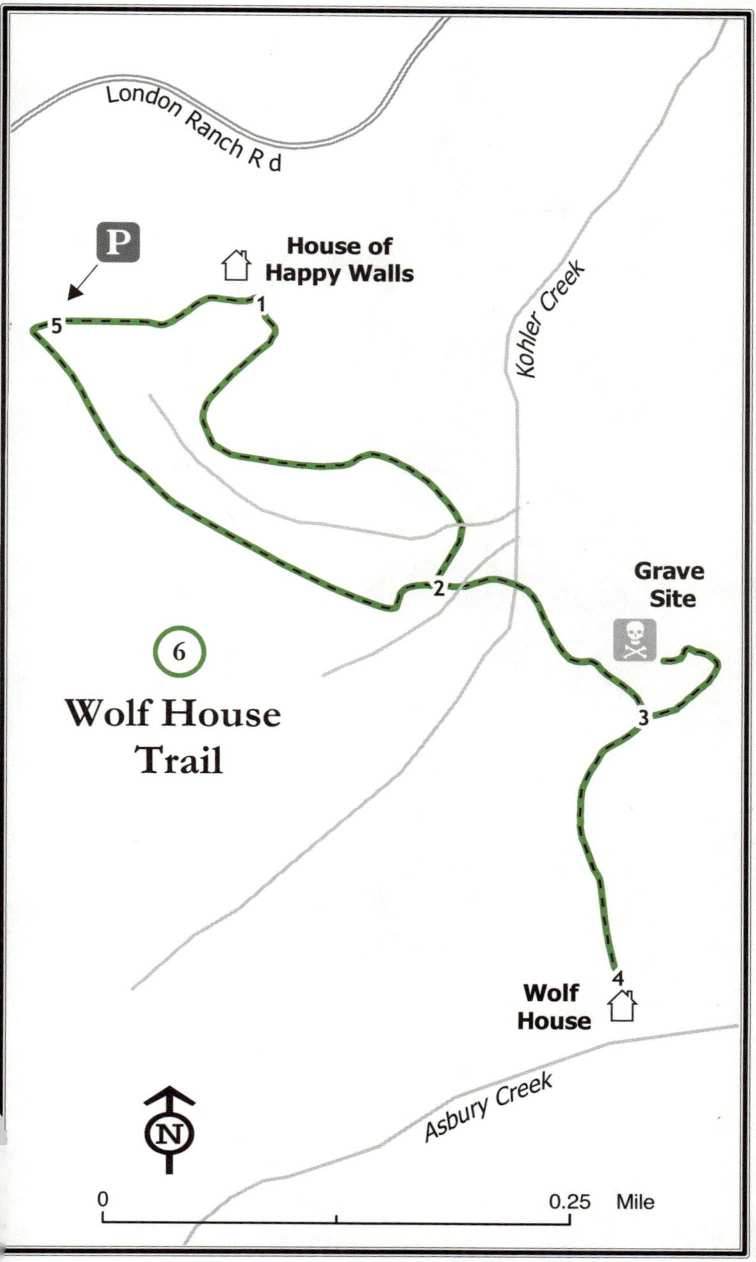
London Ranch Rd
P
House of Happy Walls
1
5
Kohler Creek
2
Grave Site
3
6
Wolf House Trail
4
Wolf House
Asbury Creek
N
0
0.25 Mile

7

Grandmother Redwood

Asbury Creek Trail

4 miles/Moderate/1 to 2 hours

This refreshing hike to the Grandmother Redwood tree in Jack London State Historic Park winds through shady redwood glens, past Jack London's lake, and across lovely Asbury Creek. An old-growth redwood in a calm grove, the tree makes a wonderful companion for lunch. If you walk quietly, you may hear the wild, laughing call of a pileated woodpecker or its deep drumming against a tree trunk. Watch and listen for other bird life as well—the Grandmother Redwood is known as an occasional resting place for owls.

A Note about this Hike: As of this writing, Jack London State Historic Park is planning some major changes in its trails. Much of the area you'll be walking through was transferred to the State Park in 2001, through the combined efforts of the Sonoma Ecology Center, Sonoma Mountain Preservation, and the Sonoma Developmental Center Parents' Group. Some of the old roads on the transferred property will eventually be converted to trails. We recommend checking with the rangers at the kiosk or park museum to see if the directions to the Grandmother Redwood have changed from the description written here.

Getting There: From Sonoma Plaza, take Highway 12 north through the Boyes Hot Springs area. After 4.5 miles, turn left on Madrone Road, where a sign reads "Sonoma Developmental Center." Follow Madrone for about 1 mile to its end, then turn right on Arnold Drive. Continue on Arnold through the campus-like setting of the developmental center and into the town of Glen Ellen. Turn left on London Ranch Road at the sign for Jack London State Historic Park. Drive up the hill to the park entrance kiosk (8.7 miles from Sonoma Plaza). After paying your entrance fee, immediately turn right up a short hill to the upper parking lot.

From the trailhead at the parking lot, follow the path up a rise to a picnic area, then down to a dirt road. Turn right on the road, passing an old stone barn and the cottage where Jack London
1 wrote many of his novels. Reaching a **vineyard**

after about 3 minutes of walking, take the road's right fork. Soon you'll pass London's cinder-block silos—cutting-edge farm architecture for 1910. The road skirts the vineyard, curving left at each corner. Here and there blackberry bushes line the road, making for a welcome snack in July and August.

A few more minutes of walking bring you to a
2 **gate** across the road and a sign reading "Lake" with arrows pointing both straight ahead and up a trail to the right. Turn right on the trail, soon passing a bench on the right, and climb the hillside through a deep, shady redwood grove.

3 At a **signed fork** for the Upper Lake Trail is another bench—stay left. About 1 mile from the beginning of your hike, the trail rejoins the
4 dirt road at the **lake**. There are picnic tables nearby.

Easy Option: Pause at the lake to rest or have a picnic lunch. Then retrace your steps to the parking lot, completing a 2-mile round trip.

Continuing on, follow the road along the base of London's stone dam. At the end of the dam the Mountain Trail takes off to the right, heading up

Sonoma Mountain (see next hike). Stay left, soon passing a wooden water tank on the left,
5 and curve downhill to a **gate** in a vineyard fence. At the gate, make a sharp right onto a footpath that follows the fence. You'll see some beautiful views over the vines to the Mayacamas, which form the opposite ridge of Sonoma Valley.

6 Coming to a **trail junction**, stay left, on the lower trail. Soon the trail becomes a dirt road again and about ½ mile from the lake comes to a gate at the former boundary of the Sonoma Developmental Center, now part of the state park. Fifty yards later you cross a tributary of Asbury Creek. In the summer this is just a trickle of water, bordered with elk clover, whose large leaves and lush foliage have an almost tropical feel. Continuing on, you enter another redwood grove, perhaps more impressive than the one below the lake.

7 A few minutes later you pass **another road** coming in from the left; stay right and more or less on level terrain. Continue until the road
8 makes a **T-intersection** with another dirt road. Turn left and walk a hundred yards, watching closely for a small trail that heads down to the right into a little hollow, where you'll find Grandmother Redwood.

Please remain outside the wooden barrier, which protects soil around the trunk from being compacted by human footsteps. Like all redwoods, this tree relies on fog drip to survive the dry summer months: moisture gleaned from ocean fog slipping over Sonoma Mountain is caught by the redwood's needles and drips to the ground, where it eventually reaches the roots of this tree. The survivor of at least one fire and several cycles of logging, the Grandmother Redwood is about 45 feet in circumference and may be over 2,000 years old. Known to some as the Saxophone Tree because of the shape of it branches, its gnarled wood probably saved it from the axes and saws that stripped Sonoma Mountain of trees in the nineteenth and early twentieth centuries.

Retrace your steps back to the parking lot.

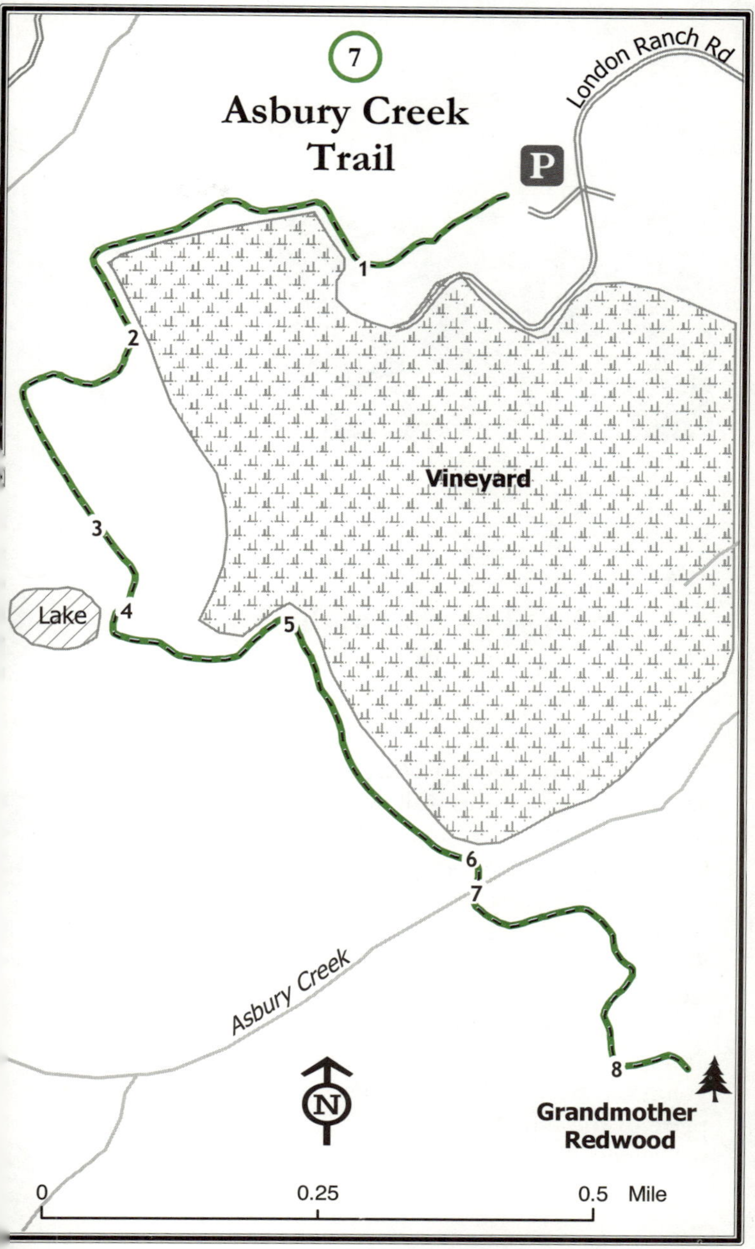
7
Asbury Creek Trail
London Ranch Rd
P
1
2
3
4
5
6
7
8
Lake
Vineyard
Asbury Creek
N
Grandmother Redwood
0
0.25
0.5 Mile

8

The Mountain of the Moon

Sonoma Ridge Trail

11 miles/Challenging/3 to 5 hours

Oak forests, redwood groves, long views, and solitude are the rewards of this walk, which takes you deep into the backcountry of upper Sonoma Mountain. The Coast Miwok people called the mountain *oona-pais;* in their creation story, it was the only place not covered by water when the world began. Geologists consider Sonoma Mountain somewhat of a puzzle, with its layers of volcanic and metamorphic rock. At one time there was even a coal mine on the eastern slope. The Sonoma Ridge Trail was constructed largely by volunteer crews led by State Park experts. It is a small piece of the Bay Area Ridge Trail, a 400-mile path that will eventually circle San Francisco Bay.

Getting There: From Sonoma Plaza, take Highway 12 north through the Boyes Hot Springs area. After 4.5 miles, turn left on Madrone Road, where a sign reads "Sonoma Developmental Center." Follow Madrone about 1 mile to its end, then turn right on Arnold Drive. Continue on Arnold through the campus-like Developmental Center and into the town of Glen Ellen. Just before the main bridge, turn left at the sign for Jack London State Historic Park. Drive up the hill to the park entrance kiosk. After paying your entrance fee, immediately turn right up a short hill to the upper parking lot.

From the trailhead at the parking lot, follow the path up a rise to a picnic area, then down to a dirt road. Turn right on the road, passing an old stone barn and the cottage where Jack London wrote many of his novels. Reaching a
1 **vineyard** after about 3 minutes of walking, take the road's right fork. Soon you pass London's twin cinderblock silos—cutting-edge farm architecture for 1910. The road skirts the vineyard, curving left at each corner. Here and there blackberry bushes line the road, making for a welcome snack in July and August.

A few minutes' walk brings you to a **metal**
2 **gate** and a sign for the lake. Arrows point both straight ahead and up a trail to the right. Turn right on the trail, soon passing a bench on the right, and continue climbing through a deep, shady redwood grove.

3 At a **signed junction** for the Upper Lake Trail is another bench, stay to the left. The trail soon
4 reaches the **lake**. There are picnic tables here

and a restroom just beyond the far end of the dam.

Following the road along the base of the dam to a signpost, stay right on the road marked "Mountain Trail." Follow the road uphill
5 above the lake and left around a **switchback** (do not take the path to the right marked with the No Bicycles symbol). After a few minutes,
6 you'll come to a clearing with a **trail junction** and a bench. If the weather is clear, there's a view all the way to Mount Diablo. The trail to the left is signed "Fallen Bridge Trail." Stay right and on the road.

Continue climbing, soon coming to another
7 **trail junction**, with a sign reading "Asbury Creek, 0.6 miles." Again, stay on the road. As you climb, the forest changes from predominately redwoods to a mix that includes madrone, oak, and bay. There are also some large Douglas fir here; if there's a breeze, pause and listen for the wind in their needles, which sounds like distant ocean breakers.

8 Pass the **junction** with Treadmill Road on the left. A little further along, the "Mountain Trail" road comes within earshot of Graham Creek; even in late summer you'll probably hear it splashing away in its shady canyon.

9 Turn left at the sign for the **Sonoma Ridge Trail**. Pause at a kiosk with a map of the trail and information about the variety of groups and individuals who worked together to create this trail.

The trail climbs to an open meadow with a view across the valley to the Mayacamas Mountains,
10 passes the other end of **Treadmill Road**, and soon brings you to a pleasant little spot in the
11 redwoods where upper **Asbury Creek** trickles over the rocks, even in September. It's a great place to rest and eat lunch.

Continuing on, the trail winds higher and higher
12 on a fairly gentle grade. You pass **viewpoints** that look across the valley and north to Mount St. Helena. Thick stands of native bunch-grasses and ferns cover the ground in many places.
13 More steady climbing leads to **vistas** south to San Pablo Bay.

Crest out at the edge of a grassy area, follow the trail to the left, and continue to the start of the **trail**
14 **loop**. Whether you go left or right, you will circle back to this point in about 10 minutes. Listen for the high, clear call of red-shouldered hawks hunting the open areas on the loop.

Returning to the beginning of the loop, retrace your steps back to the parking lot.

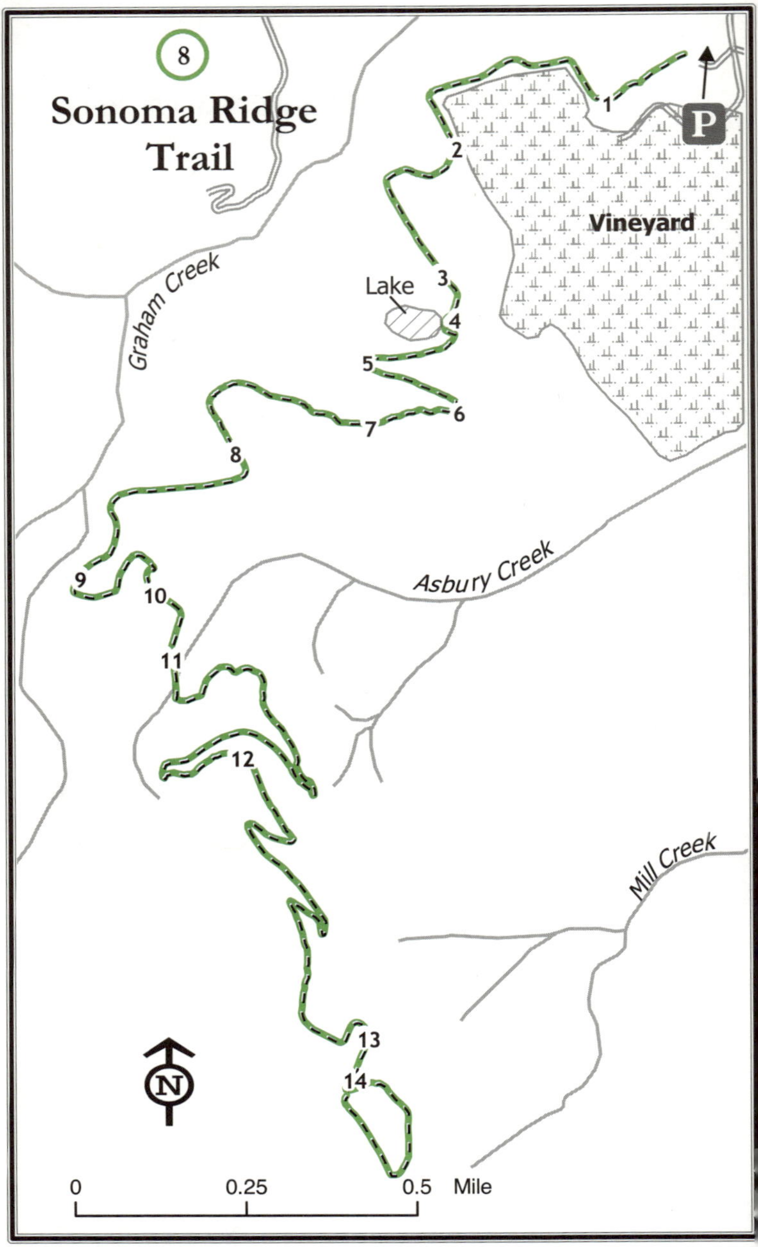

8
Sonoma Ridge Trail
Vineyard
P
Lake
Graham Creek
Asbury Creek
Mill Creek
1
2
3
4
5
6
7
8
9
10
11
12
13
14
N
0
0.25
0.5
Mile

9

Jumping Frogs

Lawndale Trail to Ledson Marsh

5 ¾ miles/Moderate/2 to 3 hours

One of the pleasures of the Lawndale Trail is the opportunity to visit many different habitats in a short distance. On hot summer days, much of its route offers a hint of the cool forests of the Pacific Northwest as it winds beneath the deep green canopy of a Douglas fir forest. You will also travel through areas of California oak woodland and patches of sunny chaparral reminiscent of southern California. The Lawndale Trail more or less follows an old route once used by stonecutters working in the basalt quarries of present-day Annadel State Park. Cobblestones from these quarries were shipped out by train and used to pave streets all over northern California. Annadel, or

"Annie's Dell," named for Anne Hutchinson whose family owned a ranch in the area, was the next station up the line from Sonoma toward Santa Rosa.

Getting There: Starting from the Sonoma Plaza, take Highway 12 north through the Boyes Hot Springs area, passing Verano Avenue, Boyes Boulevard, and Agua Caliente Roads. Pass the Glen Ellen turnoff at Arnold Drive and continue through Kenwood with its shops and restaurants. Pass Adobe Canyon Road and Hoff Road and make a left on Lawndale Road. Follow Lawndale about 2 miles to a dirt parking lot on the right.

The trail begins with a climb through an open hillside with scattered oak, buckeye, manzanita, and madrone. The ridge ahead of you is toothed with Douglas fir. The trail soon narrows and enters a mossy forest, crossing and recrossing a
1 shaded gully, gently climbing to a **knoll** with views across the valley. A path to a picnic table takes off to the left but rejoins the main trail.

Soon you'll enter a dark, cool Douglas fir forest. Sword, bracken, and five-finger ferns cover the forest floor, and in winter you may share the trail with orange-bellied newts. As you go higher, you enter redwood forest.

About halfway to the marsh, the path
2 switchbacks under **power lines**, passes briefly through a patch of scrub oaks, manzanita, and

madrone, then returns to Douglas fir and redwood. You'll cross a clearing and then pass a
3 "**borrow pit**" on the right, where the stonecutters sliced into the hillside to get to the bedrock.

Eventually the trail turns into road and comes to
4 a **four-way junction**. Continue straight ahead.

The trail is now flat, crossing a plateau with manzanitas and small oaks and glimpses of Bennett Mountain to the west. The feeling here
5 is of being in a separate world. Pass a **road** on the left with a signpost for Lawndale Trail.

6 Reach a **road junction** and turn left. In a few minutes you reach two park benches
7 and a **kiosk** at the edge of Ledson Marsh, which in the winter is a combination of open water and tules. In midsummer, it often dries up enough to walk

Extended Option: Follow the Marsh Trail along the edge of Ledson Marsh, keeping to the right at trail junctions. When you reach the Ridge Trail, follow it clockwise around the marsh until it brings you back to the Marsh Trail and the **road**
(6) **junction**. Circling the marsh will add about 5 miles to your walk.

across. Here you may see red-winged blackbirds, coots, and even a red-legged frog, the species made famous in Mark Twain's short story "The Celebrated Jumping Frog of Calaveras County."

Retrace your steps back to the parking lot.

9
Lawndale Trail
P
Lawndale Rd
Powerlines
1
2
3
4
5
6
7
Ledson Marsh
N
0
0.25
0.5 Mile

10

Time Out from the World

Pony Gate and Canyon Trail Loop

2 ¼ miles/Moderate/1 to 2 hours

Most spectacular in winter and spring, when the waterfall is running high, this walk is a year-round treat, offering an entrée to the solace and beauty of Sonoma Creek in Sugarloaf Ridge State Park. On hot summer days, the creekside woods deep in Adobe Canyon provide natural air conditioning; in winter and spring, the creek flows high and wild; in fall, yellow maple leaves drift over the path leaving a musky scent in the air. Plan to spend time on the boulders along the creek for a welcome time out from the world. This short hike has some steep sections that elevate it from an easy to a moderate hike, but the trail is well maintained and easily negotiable for most hikers.

Getting There: Starting from the Sonoma Plaza, take Highway 12 north through the Boyes Hot Springs area, passing Verano Avenue, Boyes Boulevard, and Agua Caliente Roads. Pass the Glen Ellen turnoff at Arnold Drive and continue through the town of Kenwood. Turn right on Adobe Canyon Road and follow it 3.5 miles to the entrance kiosk for Sugarloaf Ridge State Park. A day-use fee is payable at the kiosk, where rangers offer maps and park information. Continue straight about 0.1 mile to a large parking lot on the left.

From the parking lot, walk back toward the kiosk. Just before the kiosk, turn right onto
1 the Pony Gate Trail at the **trailhead**.

The Pony Gate starts out winding across open grassland and through small groves of trees. In
2 just under ¼ mile you reach a **trail junction.** Turn right and continue a short distance to a second junction with a trail heading uphill to the right. You'll see a marker here designating this section as part of the Bay Area Ridge Trail, a work-in-progress that strings together public lands encircling the San Francisco Bay. Go straight, following the Pony Gate Trail downhill, eventually entering a shady little
3 canyon and crossing a **small creek**.

4 As you reach **Adobe Canyon Road**, turn right and walk along the road for about 50 yards to

Canyon Trail. Turn left off the pavement and follow the path through Douglas fir and redwood forest. The trail soon reaches Sonoma Creek, following it upstream through the deep shade of upper Adobe Canyon.

5 A few minutes of walking bring you to an unmarked **trail junction**. Fifty yards to the right is the waterfall, which in winter and spring cascades over massive boulders. Even in early autumn, when the falls themselves are usually dry, there is a deep pool of water at the base. If you look carefully, you may see steelhead trout, which migrate from the Pacific Ocean to spawn here. Steelhead are a threatened species, and habitat restoration efforts are currently underway in Sonoma Valley. For the time being, Sonoma Creek and all its tributaries are off limits to fishing while steelhead make a comeback in our watershed. Crayfish can also be spotted in this pool.

(5) Returning from the waterfall to the **trail junction**, turn right and head uphill. This is the steepest part of the walk and there are steps among the mossy boulders to aid the ascent. The forest changes as you climb,

madrone, bay, and Douglas fir dominating more and more as you leave the moist canyon behind for the drier mountainside.

Reaching the top of the Canyon Trail, cross
6 Adobe Canyon Road to a small **dirt parking area** and another trailhead for the Pony Gate Trail. Follow this trail about ¼ mile to a
(2) **junction**, the same one you passed at the beginning of the walk. Turn right and return to
(1) the Pony Gate **trailhead** by the entrance kiosk and then up the road to the parking lot.

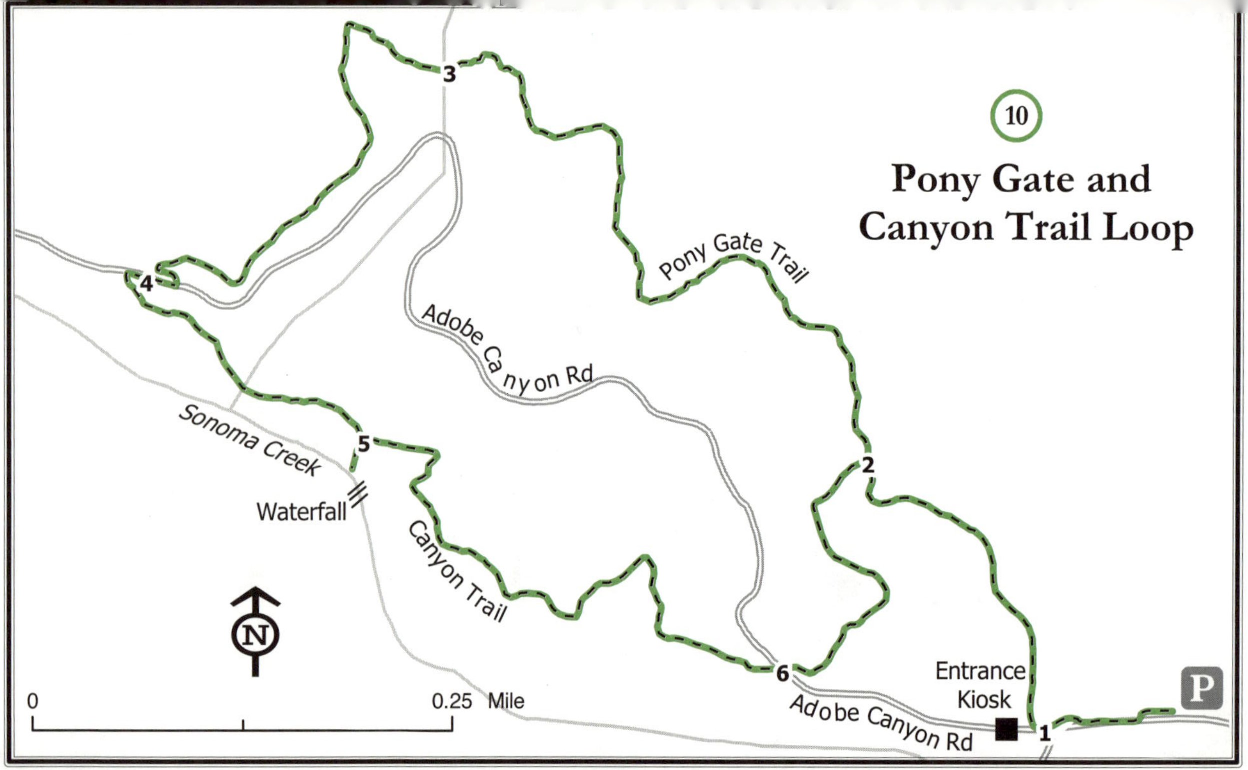

10
Pony Gate and
Canyon Trail Loop
Pony Gate Trail
Adobe Canyon Rd
Sonoma Creek
Waterfall
Canyon Trail
Entrance
Kiosk
Adobe Canyon Rd
P
N
0
0.25 Mile
1
2
3
4
5
6

11

Walking in Space

Meadow Loop and Planet Walk

2 5/8 miles/Easy to Moderate/1 to 2 hours

Offering perhaps the best family hike in the area, this walk makes a loop on the valley floor along upper Sonoma Creek in Sugarloaf Ridge State Park. It has the added attraction of following both the park's nature trail and the Planet Walk, which journeys through a scaled-down replica of the solar system. The easier version of the walk brings you as far as Saturn; ambitious walkers can continue all the way to Pluto on the park's upper rim.

Getting There: Starting from the Sonoma Plaza, take Highway 12 north through the Boyes Hot Springs area, passing Verano Avenue, Boyes Boulevard, and Agua Caliente Roads. Pass the Glen Ellen turnoff at Arnold Drive and continue through the town of Kenwood. Turn right on Adobe Canyon Road and follow it 3.5 miles to the entrance kiosk for Sugarloaf Ridge State Park. A day-use fee is payable at the kiosk, where rangers offer maps and park information. Continue straight about 0.1 mile to a large parking lot on the left.

The trail begins at the uphill corner of the parking lot, where you'll see a map kiosk. The beginning of this walk follows the Lower Bald Mountain Trail, a gentle path that traverses grassland and mixed oak and madrone woodland. Signs of coyote and other wildlife may be found, and deer frequent the meadows. Watch for tracks and the flattened, grassy bedding spots of deer families.

One-quarter mile of walking brings you to a
1 **signpost** at a fork in the path. Stay right on
the Meadow Trail. A minute later you'll reach
another fork. Again, stay right. Another ¼ mile
2 brings you to the **Ferguson Observatory**,
where there's information on the facility and a
public viewing schedule.

Across the road and to the right is the "Walk to Pluto" sign introducing the Planet Walk, with a large yellow circle representing the sun. "The Solar System is much larger and emptier than most people realize," reads the sign. "To illustrate this, we have reduced the size of the

Solar System more than two billion times to fit within the park boundaries."

Backtracking a few yards, follow the paved road past the observatory, where Mercury, Venus, and Earth are clustered in this model. You immediately come to a green gate and a sign for the Meadow Trail, actually a dirt road. A hundred yards from the Sun sign, you'll reach Mars, last of the inner planets. According to the park brochure, "With every step you take, you will cross about a million miles of empty space."

An easy walking pace propels you through the model faster than the speed of light, and in a few minutes you reach Jupiter. From an earthly perspective, the wide gravel road leads through oak-bay-madrone woodland with the upper reach of Sonoma Creek to your right. Soon you reach Saturn and a few minutes later a shady nook with picnic tables.

Easy Option: Pause at this lovely spot to rest or have a picnic lunch. Then retrace your steps to the parking lot, completing a 2 ¼-mile round trip.

3 Crossing over **Sonoma Creek** on a bridge, continue on the Meadow Trail. Pass the Gray Pine Trail on your left just before reaching
4 the **junction** with the Brushy Peaks Trail on the left.

Extended Option: Turn onto the Brushy Peaks Trail for a steep climb to outstanding views and a visit to the outer solar system.

1/8 mile to the planet Uranus
1 mile beyond Uranus to Neptune
7/8 mile from Neptune to Pluto

A trip to Pluto and back will add 4 challenging miles to your walk.

From the Brushy Peaks Trail junction, follow the Hillside Trail, which climbs out of the meadow, rewarding you with views down into the park. Reach the high point near some
5 **water tanks** and begin descending, passing horsetails and blackberry bushes (ripe in August and September).

A few more minutes of walking bring you to a junction with the park's nature trail on the left.

6 Continue on a hundred yards to a **second junction** also signed "Nature Trail." Turn left on the nature trail and follow it along Sonoma Creek for ½ mile back to the parking lot.

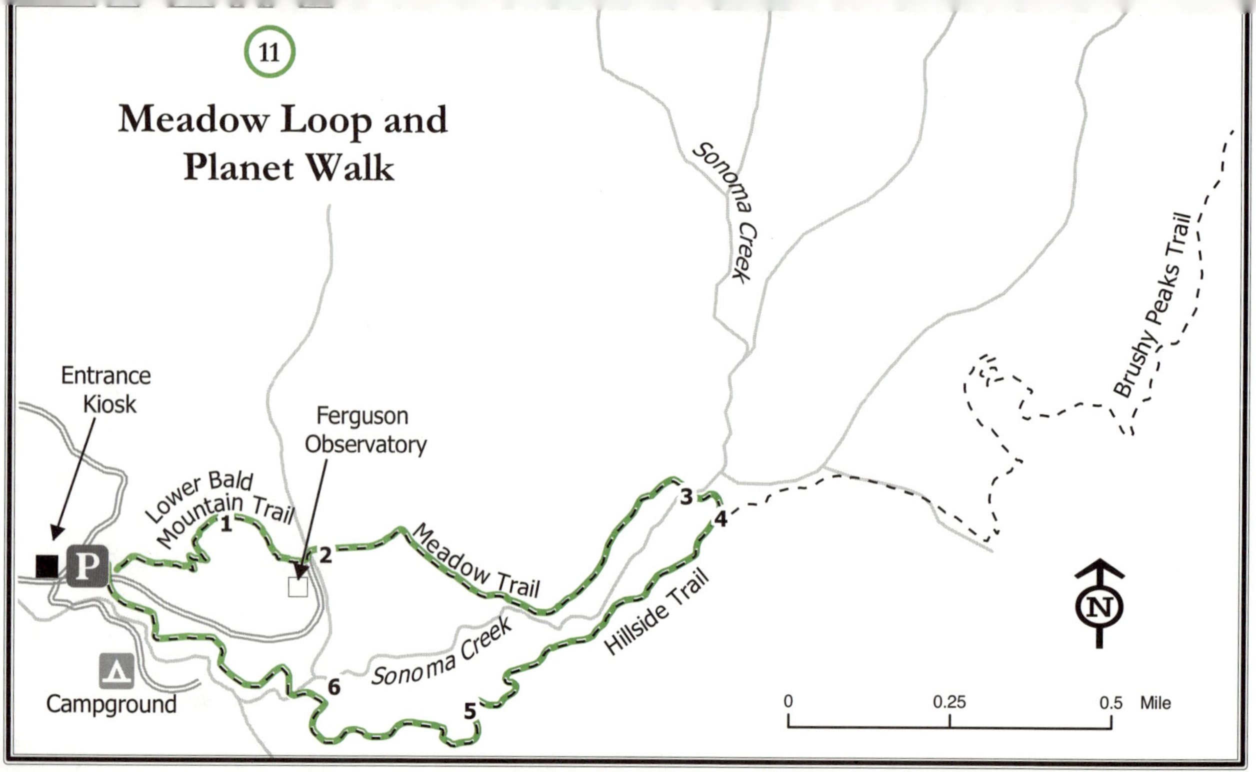
11
Meadow Loop and Planet Walk
Entrance Kiosk
Ferguson Observatory
Lower Bald Mountain Trail
Meadow Trail
Sonoma Creek
Sonoma Creek
Hillside Trail
Brushy Peaks Trail
Campground
P
1
2
3
4
5
6
N
0
0.25
0.5 Mile

12

You Can See for Miles and Miles

Bald Mountain Loop

7 ¼ mile round-trip/Challenging/3 hours

The view from the summit of Bald Mountain is one of the most spectacular in the north bay, taking in everything from the Golden Gate Bridge towers to Mt. St. Helena and beyond. Layers of ridgeline are stacked in all directions, each one growing bluer with distance as they approach the horizon. On winter days when recent storms have washed the sky to crystal, you can see 10,000-foot Pyramid Peak in the Sierra Nevada near Lake Tahoe, 129 miles away! Although Bald Mountain's elevation is a modest 2,729 feet, this trail offers a good workout as it winds upward through open meadows, oak and bay woodland, and chaparral.

This hike is best in the cool months or in early morning before the heat of a summer day. The route to the top is fairly shady; the shorter descent is much more open and exposed to the sun. If you happen to get caught in the heat, finish your visit to the park with a side trip to Sonoma Creek to cool your feet.

Getting There: Starting from the Sonoma Plaza, take Highway 12 north through the Boyes Hot Springs area, passing Verano Avenue, Boyes Boulevard, Agua Caliente Road, Madrone Road, and Arnold Drive. Continue through Kenwood, with its shops and restaurants. Turn right on Adobe Canyon Road and follow it for 3.5 miles to the entrance kiosk for Sugarloaf Ridge State Park. A day-use fee is payable here, where rangers offer maps and park information. Continue 0.1 mile straight past the kiosk to a large parking lot on the left side of the road.

The trail begins at the uphill corner of the parking lot, where you'll see a map kiosk. Follow the Lower Bald Mountain Trail, a gentle path that traverses grassland and mixed oak and madrone woodland. Signs of coyote and other wildlife may be found, and deer frequent the meadows. Watch for tracks and the flattened, grassy bedding spots of deer families.

One-quarter mile of walking brings you to a
1 **signpost**. Stay right (although the left fork
reads "Lower Bald Mountain Trail," staying
right offers a much more pleasant route to the
2 top). A minute later you reach another **fork**.
Again, stay right. Another ¼ mile brings you

3 to the **Ferguson Observatory**, where there's
information on the facility and viewing times.

Just beyond the observatory, you'll find the
beginning of the Meadow Trail (actually a dirt
road). Follow the Meadow Trail ¾ mile along
4 the valley floor and across a **bridge** over
5 Sonoma Creek to a **junction** with the Gray
Pine Trail. Turn left on the Gray Pine Trail
(also a dirt road), soon rockhopping across
Sonoma Creek. A few minutes' walk brings
6 you to **another junction** with the Vista Trail.

Turn left on the Vista Trail, which soon comes
to a small stream (still running in October at
the time of this writing) and follows it
upstream for a short distance. Beginning to
7 climb, the trail skirts **Columbine Meadow**
8 and about ½ mile later comes to a **junction**
with the Headwaters Trail.

Turn right on the Headwaters Trail, soon
passing through a mossy boulder field under
the trees and then up a shady ravine. After ½
9 mile you reach the **junction** with the Red
Mountain Trail.

Turn right on the Red Mountain Trail.
Another ½ mile brings you to a bridge over a
10 tiny **stream**, which you may find running even
if you make this hike late in the dry season.
The Red Mountain Trail switchbacks up to a
ridgeline and continues fairly level along the
mountainside. This section can be a little
brushy where the trail cuts through stands of

chaparral. A little less than ½ mile from the
11 bridge, you come back to the **Gray Pine Trail**
(still a dirt fire road).

Turn left on the Gray Pine Trail, following it up the ridgeline toward the top of Bald Mountain. Just below the summit, the Gray Pine Trail veers right. Go left on the short spur
12 to the **summit**, where there's a bench and
signs to help you identify distant mountains and other features of the view.

When you're ready to head down, turn left on the Gray Pine Trail. Almost immediately you reach a junction with the Bald Mountain Trail, another dirt road. Turn left on the Bald Mountain Trail, soon descending steeply. One-half mile from the summit you reach a notch
13 and a **junction** with a road leading to the radio
towers on top of Red Mountain.

Continue on the Bald Mountain Trail, now a paved road. Continuing down, you pass the junction with the
14 **Red Mountain**
Trail on the left and then another
15 with the **Vista**
Trail. A few minutes later you reach the junction
16 with the **Lower**
Bald Mountain Trail.

(1) Turning left on the Lower Bald Mountain Trail, descend through chaparral, oak, and madrone to the **signpost** you passed at the beginning of the walk. Turn right, staying on Lower Bald Mountain Trail, soon reaching the parking lot.

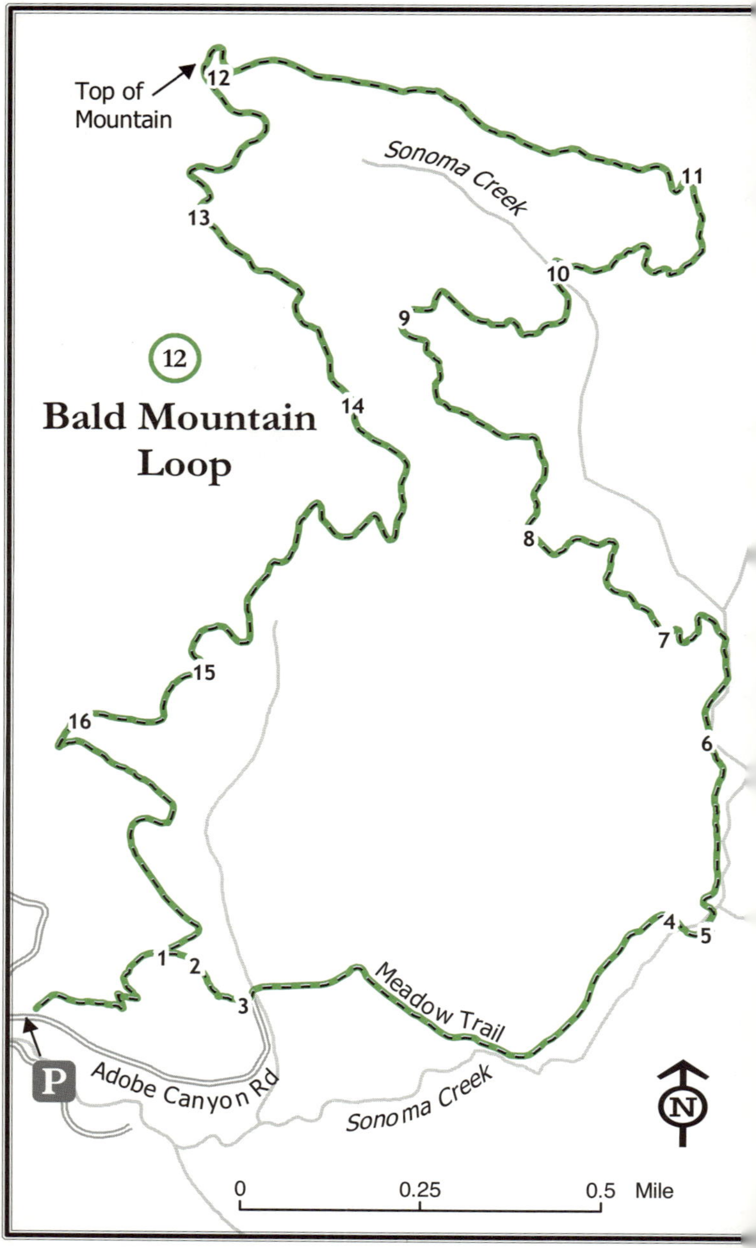

12
Bald Mountain Loop
Top of Mountain
Sonoma Creek
Meadow Trail
Adobe Canyon Rd
Sonoma Creek
P
N
1
2
3
4
5
6
7
8
9
10
11
12
13
14
15
16
0
0.25
0.5 Mile

Gunsight Rock: A Brief Description

Goodspeed/Natt Kemper Trail

7 miles/Challenging/4 to 6 hours

The trek to Gunsight Rock, high on the side of Hood Mountain, is one of Sonoma Valley's premier hikes. It is the only walk in this book that comes close to traveling all the way from valley floor to ridgetop. As a consequence, sections of the trail are quite steep and the total climb is about 2,000 vertical feet. But the effort is well worth it; from Gunsight Rock's airy perch, the entire sweep of Sonoma Valley from Kenwood to San Pablo Bay lies at your feet.

At the time we began writing this book, a landslide had closed the trail, and it was uncertain when it would reopen. Reluctantly, we decided to omit Gunsight Rock from the book. State Park staff accomplished the necessary reconstruction with impressive speed, and by the time this book was ready to go to press the trail had been reopened. Because of the timing, it wasn't possible to give this hike a full write-up with a map. However, the trail is straightforward and well-marked, and moderately experienced hikers should have no difficulty finding their way using this short description.

Getting There: Starting from the Sonoma Plaza, take Highway 12 north through the Boyes Hot Springs area, passing Verano Avenue, Boyes Boulevard, Agua Caliente Road, Madrone Road, and Arnold Drive. Continue through Kenwood, with its shops and restaurants. Turn right on Adobe Canyon Road. Follow it past houses and then a sign for Sugarloaf Ridge State Park. About 2.1 miles from Highway 12 turn into a parking lot on the left. The trail begins at the back corner of the parking lot.

Distances marked in parentheses are cumulative.

Cross Sonoma Creek on a footbridge and follow the trail a short distance to a second bridge over Bear Creek. The trail climbs through trees and open chaparral to a road (0.9 miles).

Cross the road and descend to a small, steep creek (1.1 miles). Rock-hop across the creek and begin climbing again through the forest and some open areas. Cross another stream (1.9 miles), much smaller than the last and sometimes dry in the summer.

The trail crosses an open grassy hillside with spectacular views. Pass a bench and a sign marking this section as the "Natt Kemper Trail" (2.1 miles).

Continue climbing to a notch (3.0 miles) with views over the Santa Rosa Plain, then ever upward to Pine Flat (3.3 miles). Turn left at the junction here, toward Gunsight Rock (turning right takes you to the top of Hood Mountain, which, because of trees, has virtually no view).

A short, fairly level stroll brings you to Gunsight Rock (3.5 miles), with its stunning views and distinctive rock formations. If you're lucky you may see kestrels playing here, making spectacular dives hundreds of feet straight down alongside the cliffs.

Retrace your steps to the parking lot (7.0 miles).

WALKS IN APPROXIMATE ORDER OF DIFFICULTY

WALK#	DISTANCE	TERRAIN
6	1 3/8 miles	Almost level
3	2 ¼ miles	Level
1	2 ½ miles	Level
11	2 5/8 miles	Some hills
10	2 ¼ miles	Hilly
2	2 7/8 miles	Hilly
5	3 miles	Hilly
7	4 miles	Hilly
9	5 ¾ miles	Hilly
4	8 1/8 miles	Level
12	7 ¼ miles	Steep
Gunsight Rock	7 miles	Steep
8	11 miles	Steep

Easy Options in green text boxes describe shorter versions of these walks:

Walk 1	1 7/8 miles	Level
Walk 4	5 ½ miles	Level
Walk 5	¼ to 2 ½ miles	Almost level
Walk 7	2 miles	Hilly
Walk 11	2 ¼ miles	Level

Extended Options, also in green text boxes, describe longer versions of these walks:

Walk 1	6 ½ miles	Level & hilly
Walk 3	3 to 6 ¼ miles	Level
Walk 9	10 ¾ miles	Hilly
Walk 11	6 5/8 miles	Steep

About the Authors

Rebecca Lawton, a geologist and former whitewater guide, is the author of *Reading Water: Lessons from the River* (Capital, 2002) and *Discover Nature in the Rocks* (Stackpole, 1997). She lives in Sonoma with her daughter, Rose.

Arthur Dawson, world traveler, poet, teacher, and historical ecologist, is the author of *The Stories Behind Sonoma Valley Place Names* (Kulupi, 1998), *Creek Wisdom: An Ecological History of Sonoma Valley as told by local elders* (Kulupi, 2003), and other publications. He lives in Glen Ellen with his wife, Jill, and their two children, Kyrie and Larkin.

Kulupi Press

Founded in 1998, Kulupi Press is dedicated to deepening and enriching its readers' sense of place. Its first publication, *The Stories Behind Sonoma Valley Place Names*, was a local bestseller and held the #1 position on Amazon.com's "Bestseller, Santa Rosa" list for more than 3 years.

For more information on Kulupi's current offerings, contact us at www.kulupi.com or the old-fashioned way:

Kulupi Press
5026 Warm Springs Road
Glen Ellen, CA 95442
(707) 996-8727

Ryno Mapping

For information about mapping and cartographic services available from Ryno Mapping, go to www.rynomapping.com or send an e-mail to ryan@rynomapping.com.